CONS'

C000219905

A Life from Beginning to End

Copyright © 2021 by Hourly History.

Table of Contents

Introduction

Emperor Constantine I came into this world on February 27, 272 CE, with the elaborate name of Flavius Valerius Constantinus. His city of birth was a place called Naissus, which is now part of Serbia but then formed part of the Roman Empire. It's fitting that the man who would usher in the greatness of the Eastern Roman Empire would start his life in the Balkan regions of southeastern Europe.

Constantine's father, Constantius Chlorus, was a soldier serving under Emperor Aurelian's official guard and was steadily rising through the ranks. He was highly influential to the future politics of Constantine, as it was through his father's legacy that Constantine would one day rise up to become Roman emperor. On the other hand, it was Constantine's mother Helena who would influence Constantine's religious sentiments since it was from her that he would learn of a growing religious sect known as Christianity.

At the time of Constantine's adolescence, the Roman Empire was at a crossroads. The territory of the empire itself had become so large that it was becoming increasingly difficult for just one person to govern. This difficulty led then-Emperor Diocletian to split the administration of the empire between four rulers which would form what was known as the Tetrarchy, or the "rule of four."

The Tetrarchy was a system of governance that evolved into having Diocletian as the senior emperor of the eastern half of the empire and his former subordinate, Maximian, as ruler of the western half. Both Diocletian and Maximian also had a junior partner who was referred to as a *caesar* aiding them in their administration—Galerius in the east and Constantius Chlorus in the west. Constantius Chlorus was, of course, none other than the father of Constantine.

From this potent mixture of Constantius' strong political ties and Helena's religious faith, the world would eventually get Emperor Constantine the Great.

Chapter One

Groomed for the Throne

"It is by the exercise of right understanding and sound discretion, that we are enabled really to enjoy our blessings."

—Constantine the Great

Diocletian's decision to divide the Roman Empire into a Tetrarchy was a fateful one, and initially, it seemed to have been quite successful in its goal of better streamlining Roman authority. The days of an emperor having to rush from one side of the empire to the other in order to face imminent threats were over. With clear communication between the four rulers, any external threat against the empire could be quickly addressed.

As a result, it is generally agreed that by the end of the third century CE, the Roman Empire was a largely stable dominion. This stability, however, depended upon the four rulers of the

Tetrarchy being able to get along with each other, and that was most certainly not guaranteed. The subordinate caesars especially were constantly trying to ingratiate themselves with their senior emperor, or *augustus*.

Constantius Chlorus, for his part, was eager to get into the good graces of the western emperor, Maximian. So, when the opportunity came to marry his daughter Theodora, he jumped at the chance. In the politics of those days, marriages of political convenience were quite common, and it was believed that marriage was an excellent way to shore up the bonds of political partners. The only trouble, of course, was that Constantius was already married.

The record isn't entirely clear if Constantius officially divorced Constantine's mother Helena or just quietly put her to the side, but she most certainly was made to take a backseat once Constantius acquired his new wife. Constantius had by no means abandoned his son, however, and still considered him to be his future successor. Constantius was, in fact, busily grooming Constantine and giving him advice. Shortly after marrying Theodora, Constantius even suggested that his son marry his wife's younger sister, Fausta. Such a union would have made father and son brothers-in-law. Constantine firmly rejected the offer, but as fate would have it, he would come to marry Fausta later on.

At any rate, as much as Constantius Chlorus hoped that shoring up his relations with the western emperor would improve his status in the short term, it managed to provoke the suspicion of the eastern emperor Diocletian. Diocletian became concerned over the solidarity that was developing in the western block of the empire between Constantius and Maximian. It was for this reason that he requested that Constantius' son Constantine come live with him at his base of operations in Nicomedia in the eastern half of the Roman Empire (modern-day Turkey). Constantine essentially became a royal hostage of Diocletian's, held just in case the western rulers got any ideas of overstepping their authority.

This move would mean that Constantine would grow up quite familiar with the eastern part of the Roman Empire. Having that said, it's really no wonder that he would later make his grand capital of Constantinople in the east since that was where his heart belonged. Constantine understood the glorious past of Rome, but he couldn't help but feel that the empire's true future was in the eastern frontiers, to which he would grow so accustomed.

Constantine was brought up and trained by both the junior Caesar Galerius, as well as by Diocletian himself. By 296 CE, he was already heading out on expeditions with the Roman army—first against barbarians on the Danube River and then against the Persians in Syria. In the meantime, his father was also sent out to war as he tackled a rebellion taking place in Gaul (modern-day France) in the western half of the empire. This fight would ultimately lead all the way to Britain before the revolt was finally quashed by Constantius.

Happy with how things were going in the Roman government, Diocletian made it known that he eventually intended for Maximian to be succeeded by Constantine's father Constantius Chlorus and, in the east, for Diocletian himself to be succeeded by his own caesar, Galerius. This determination appeared to lay the groundwork for Constantine himself to become a caesar and then eventually a Roman emperor.

Constantine made his way back from the fighting in the east in 303 CE, just in time to see what would become known as the Great Persecution erupt against the Christians of the

Roman Empire. Diocletian is known as the last Roman Emperor to actively go after Christians, and it is somewhat fitting that Constantine—the future emperor and Christian champion—would have first-hand knowledge of such a devastating event.

One of the first major instances of this anti-Christian pogrom occurred in the spring of 303 when Diocletian instructed his legions of troops to set the new Christian Church in Nicomedia ablaze. This was one of the main focal points of Christianity in the east, and by leveling it to the ground, Diocletian was sending out a message to Christians everywhere that the Roman Empire was actively trying to shut them down.

The burning down of the Nicomedia Church was followed by several other churches being seized and demolished. With their churches abolished, priests then had their ranks revoked, and more often than not, they were thrown in jail. Although Constantine would later try to claim that he was an opponent of Diocletian's attack on the church, there is no evidence to suggest that he spoke out against it at the time.

At the very least, Constantine appears to have been a silent bystander who allowed the destruction to take place without any interference.

In truth, however, there was certainly very little that Constantine could have done, even if he had tried. If he had gone against Diocletian's edicts, he would have been immediately punished for his actions—punishment that would have ended Constantine's career, if not his life. If Constantine had taken a strong stand against Diocletian's Great Persecution, there most likely would have never been an Emperor Constantine, and without his ascension to the throne, Rome's later acceptance of the Christian faith would be much more uncertain.

As it turns out, this persecution of Christians ended up being Diocletian's last major act as emperor. Shortly thereafter, in the winter of 304, he became seriously ill, and the following year, he announced his intention to resign. Some Christians—relieved that their persecution seemed to be at an end—no doubt took this as an answer to their prayers. At any rate, with Diocletian stepping down from the imperial throne, the question then remained as to who would succeed him.

The most obvious solution would have been to have the two caesars—Galerius in the east and Constantius Chlorus in the west—promoted to senior emperors. Many assumed that Constantius' son Constantine would then be made a caesar of the west, but this was not the case. Instead, Flavius Valerius Severus, an officer of the Roman armed forces, was made Constantius' caesar, while Maximinus Daia—Galerius' nephew—was promoted to caesar under Galerius.

Constantine had been apparently passed over for this most coveted of promotions. It was a devastating blow, but soon enough, the winds of fate would shift once again—and this time in Constantine's favor.

Chapter Two

How the Roman West was Won

"Beginning from the very borders of the ocean, I have aroused each nation of the world in succession to a well-grounded hope of security; so that those which, groaning in servitude to the most cruel tyrants and yielding to the pressure of their daily sufferings, had well nigh been utterly destroyed, have been restored through my agency to a far happier state."

—Constantine the Great

After the resignation of Diocletian, the Roman Empire received an update to its Tetrarchy. Constantine's father, Constantius Chlorus, would be the senior emperor of the west with Severus as his subordinate caesar. In the east, Galerius was made senior emperor with his nephew Maximinus Daia serving as his caesar. Young Constantine initially remained in the east, even though the governance of Galerius and Maximinus was becoming increasingly hostile toward him. There was even talk of potential plots being hatched threatening Constantine's life.

Nevertheless, Constantine's father was now the emperor of the west, so obviously he still had some major clout at his disposal. It was, in fact, his father that insisted that Constantine be sent over to his side of the empire so that he could help him fight a campaign in the British Isles against a tribe of Picts. There was some pushback from Galerius, who feared that Constantine was too popular to be let loose unchaperoned, but eventually, after a night of drinking, Galerius gave in to the pressure and allowed the young Constantine to travel to the west to be with his father.

So it was that Constantine and his father crossed paths once again, meeting up in the port of Boulogne in modern-day France in the year 305 CE. From here, they hopped on a ship and headed across the English Channel to oversee the fight against the Picts. Perhaps besides wishing for his son to help him with the military campaign, Constantius also simply wanted to see his son one more time. Because as it turned out, Constantius' days were numbered.

Shortly after getting to see his son one last time, Constantius' health failed him, and he died on July 25, 306 CE. Some accounts say that Constantius declared Constantine his successor right before his death, while others state that it was his soldiers who unanimously proclaimed it right after he passed.

Whatever the case may be, the idea of Constantine automatically becoming emperor of the west was not something that the eastern Emperor Galerius was willing to accept. He soon made it known that Constantius' former caesar, Severus, would be the one to succeed Constantius. Constantine was, however, granted the title of caesar under the leadership of Severus.

In reality, this was not a bad position for Constantine to be in at the time. He was still a relatively young man, and by being caesar, he could learn the ropes while leaving the main authority in the hands of Severus. A smooth transition was not to be though, since Maxentius, son of the former Emperor Maximian, suddenly caught everyone by surprise by cobbling together a group of supporters and seizing the Roman capital by force.

Now there were two supposed emperors of the West—Severus and Maxentius—with

Constantine as caesar. This situation obviously needed to be addressed. It was Galerius who immediately called upon Severus to send in the troops and take Rome back from Maxentius. With a large army at his disposal, it seemed like it should have been a relatively easy operation to root out Maxentius. But when push came to shove, Maxentius surprised everyone by beseeching his father—the then-retired emperor—Maximian.

In his hour of need, Maxentius managed to convince his father to reclaim his role as emperor. Maximian accepted the offer, and soon Severus had massive defection of the ranks, as soldiers who still felt loyal to the former Emperor Maximian deserted him and flocked to Rome. Maximian then managed to convince Severus himself to abandon his role and resign from his position.

With only the little Caesar Constantine standing in Maximian's way of total domination of the western half of the empire, the eastern Emperor Galerius tried to send in more troops to take down Maximian. He was unable to do so, and in the aftermath, Severus—who had previously been promised a safe retirement—was put to death by Maximian. This was no doubt done to eliminate the possibility of having Severus put back on the throne.

With only Constantine left in his way, Maximian decided to use diplomacy on the caesar. He proposed that Constantine join forces with him. Constantine, probably figuring his options were rather limited, agreed. To further their bond, Constantine wed Maximian's daughter, Fausta. This agreement left the western half of the empire as a continually disputed territory between three powerful figures— Maximian, Maxentius, and Constantine. At one point, Maxentius even fled to Constantine for aid after having a falling out with his father.

Even more drama erupted in 310 CE when Maximian tried to take down Constantine with military force. These efforts ultimately failed, and after he was stripped of all his titles, Maximian allegedly used a rope to commit suicide. After his father's demise, Maxentius was not destined to remain in Constantine's good graces either, and by 312, the two were leading factions against each other.

Constantine sent an army through the Alps in the northern reaches of the Italian peninsula in hot pursuit of his rival. He soon readily handed defeat to Maxentius' troops. This victory led to the final face-off between the two men, which occurred on the Milvian Bridge on the outskirts of Rome. It would be this one battle that would decide everything; the victor would be the unquestioned ruler of the western half of the empire.

Considering the high stakes involved, Constantine was obviously under a lot of pressure to ensure his troops succeeded. Immediately before this crucial battle, Constantine allegedly had a supernatural vision. In the vision, he was told to put the sign of the Christian cross on the shields of his troops. Although his mother was a Christian, Constantine was pagan. The idea of him bearing the symbol of the cross was a strange concept for him, but according to legend, after the vision, he readily obeyed the instructions.

Roman chronicler Eusebius offered a slightly different variation of these events, claiming that Constantine, as well as many of his troops, saw something quite miraculous on their way to Rome just before the Battle of the Milvian Bridge. They allegedly saw a fiery cross hovering above them, and upon this cross, they could clearly read the emblazoned words, "*In Hoc Signo Vinces*," which is Latin for, "In this sign, you shall conquer."

Regardless of exactly how he was inspired to do so, Constantine did indeed order his troops to decorate their shields with the sign of the cross just before the battle commenced. The following day, on October 28, 312, Constantine's forces crashed headlong into Maxentius' army. Since Constantine's army was outnumbered two-to-one, many prognosticated that he would be defeated. But just as the vision had assured him, Constantine's troops not only prevailed but utterly vanquished the troops of Maxentius. Maxentius ended up perishing with his doomed troops, and after the battle, his head was paraded through the streets for all to see.

Constantine was now the sole authority in the western half of the empire, but although he had won the west, he would still face a serious challenge from the emperor of the east.

Chapter Three

Becoming Constantine the Great

"With free minds, all are to worship their Gods."

—Constantine the Great

For several years, Constantine had had an uneasy relationship with his partner in the east, Emperor Galerius. But by 311 CE, Galerius began to have health problems and, sensing that his time on this earth was coming to a close, he began to think very deeply about past actions of imperial rule. He seemed to regret the persecutions against Christians in particular, and it was with this growing sentiment that he hammered out the so-called Edict of Toleration—an edict which, just as the title implies, decreed that Christians should be tolerated. This was not something Galerius had decided in the spur of the moment, and the words of his declaration made clear just how much thought he had given to the issue.

The edict declared, "Amongst our other measures for the advantage of the Empire, we have hitherto endeavored to bring all things into conformity with the ancient laws and public order of the Romans. We have been especially anxious that even the Christians, who have abandoned the religion of their ancestors, should return to reason. . . . Nevertheless, since many of them have continued to persist in their opinions . . . We, with our wonted clemency, have judged it wise to extend a pardon even to these men and permit them once more to become Christians and re-establish their places of meeting; in such manner; however, that they shall in no way offend against good order. Wherefore it should be the duty of the Christians, in view of our clemency, to pray to their god for our welfare, for that of the Empire, and for their own, so that the Empire may remain intact in all its parts, and that they themselves may live safely in their habitations."

The words of Galerius are intriguing because they provide us with a direct window into the layered complexity of viewpoints among Romans in regard to Christians and the status quo of the empire at the time. Galerius mentions how it was the desire of Roman authority to have conformity within the empire, with everyone observing ancient laws and customs, so that a general feeling of unity could prevail amongst the wide-ranging provinces of the empire.

Galerius then expresses concern about how the Christians had "abandoned the religion of their ancestors" and how he and other Roman authority figures had long hoped that they would "return to reason." In Galerius' day, Christianity was still considered to be a Jewish sect that had broken off from mainstream Judaism. Even though Rome encouraged the worship of traditional Roman gods, the Romans were usually tolerant of what they viewed to be "ancestral religions" of subject peoples. Christianity, having sprung from Judaism, simply did not meet that standard in Rome's eyes. The Romans long viewed the Christians as a troublesome, radical offshoot of Judaism, and as Galerius put it, they had often longed for the Christians to go back to the Jewish faith of their ancestors.

At this point though, Galerius acknowledged the reality of the situation since Christianity was continuing to grow and called for a general amnesty of Christian practitioners as long as they did not "offend good order" and as long as these Christians wished for the wellbeing of Rome. These words are important too since they seem to highlight an event that allegedly kicked off Diocletian's Great Persecution in the first place.

It has been said that while visiting Nicomedia, Diocletian heard reports of a Christian deacon who disrupted a Roman civil court where pagan sacrifices were taking place, loudly denouncing the ceremony. Diocletian despised the Christians, and disruptions like these gave him an excuse to launch an attack against them. In the aftermath of all that had transpired, Galerius came to the conclusion that Christians would be tolerated on the condition that they did not disrupt the civil affairs of Rome in the future. This would prove to be Galerius' last act because just a few days after issuing the Edict of Toleration, he passed away. The man to next seize control of the eastern half of the empire was one of Galerius' old military companions, Valerius Licinianus Licinius.

Emperor Licinius watched while the previous Tetrarchy crumbled to dust, leaving just him and Constantine as the dueling authorities of the Roman Empire. The two emperors held a meeting in Milan in 313 in order to sort out the future of the empire. Here, it was determined among other things that Licinius would marry Constantine's sister Constantia. Once again, it was hoped that the bonds of family would prevail over imperial intrigue, helping the two emperors to forge a lasting alliance with each other.

It was also in Milan that the two emperors would build upon the late Galerius' previous Edict of Toleration by forging the Edict of Milan, which went so far as to grant complete tolerance of all Christians in all parts of the Roman Empire. This was a major milestone for Christianity. Now Christianity could be practiced in the open and spread far and wide, without any fear of reprisal. The edict also included a provision that allowed Christians to retake any property that had been confiscated during the last persecution waged against them under Diocletian.

For all of the goodwill that had been worked out in Milan, however, much of it would be quickly lost. Shortly thereafter, Constantine was subjected to an attempt on his life, and the assassin was traced right back to Licinius. As tensions continued to grow, the two emperors ended up facing off against each other in 316 at the Battle of Cibalae. Despite being outnumbered, Constantine got the better of Licinius in this engagement.

The two would then have a rematch in 317 in the Battle of Mardia, and this time Licinius was forced to negotiate. In the aftermath of the battle, it was decided that Constantine's two sons—Constantine II and Crispus would be made caesars, subordinate to Constantine. It was also determined that Licinius' heir Licinianus would also be made a caesar, subordinate to Licinius.

This state of affairs held for the next few years, but in 320, it began to unravel when Licinius decided to go back on the tenants of the Edict of Milan and cause problems for Christian believers in his realm. Suddenly, Christian priests were being pushed out of office, churches were shut down, and Christian properties were seized. Part of the reason this was done was to undermine one of Constantine's main constituencies since Christians in general were highly supportive of Constantine.

Constantine, for his part, wasn't going to take such things lying down, and soon the empire was once again in a state of civil war. The war was very much one with religious implications. Licinius was not a Christian and upheld the traditional Roman pagan beliefs. His army in the east also relied heavily on pagan mercenaries, who eschewed Christianity. Constantine, on the other hand, although not officially converted to Christianity, embraced the symbolism of it and encouraged his troops to do so as well, just as they had done during the Battle of the Milvian Bridge.

In the end, Constantine and his troops were the winners in this cataclysmic struggle and soundly defeated the forces of Licinius at the Battle of Adrianople in 324 in modern-day Turkey. Licinius was forced to flee lest he be captured, and in his absence, he made one of his senior advisors, Martinian, stand in for him as a substitute emperor. Then, after decisive defeats by Constantine's army at the Battle of the Hellespont and then the Battle of Chrysopolis, both Martinian and Licinius decided that it was in their best interest to surrender.

The terms of the surrender guaranteed that they would not be treated harshly and would be allowed to retire in peace. Constantine decided to go back on this pledge, however, when Licinius allegedly attempted to assassinate him. This led to both Licinius and Martinian being seized and executed in 325. Licinius' son (and Constantine's nephew by way of his sister Constantia) was likewise killed in 326.

Constantine the Great—as he now was undoubtedly considered—was from here on out the sole authority of the Roman Empire.

Chapter Four

Unifying the Empire

*"This is certainly the Will of the Supreme God,
who is the Author of this world and its Father . . .
that the whole human race should agree together
and be joined in a certain affectionate union by,
as it were, a mutual embrace."*

—Constantine the Great

Upon attaining supreme authority over the entire
Roman Empire, Constantine sought to create a
new capital. Diocletian had previously made
Nicomedia the capital of the east, and Constantine
seems to have initially considered remaking
Nicomedia in his own image. In the end though,
he changed his mind and headed to the ancient
Greek town of Byzantium instead.

Byzantium was a Greek colony situated right
next to the Bosporus Strait on the tiny strip of
land connecting Asia to Europe. Constantine
realized that the site would be perfect for an
impenetrable imperial fortress of a capital since it

was surrounded by water on two sides and a very narrow piece of land on the other two. This would make an invasion by land very difficult since large armies would be bottle-necked when approaching the city.

The location was also convenient because it would allow for the creation of powerful ports from which ships could be quickly launched across the Mediterranean Sea to just about any other vital hub of the empire. Constantine called his city *Nova Roma Constantinopolitana*, or as it would be in plain English, the New Rome of Constantinople. He envisioned it to be the new Rome, and in many ways, it was indeed like an updated version of the old city.

Interestingly enough, the city rested upon seven hills, just as Rome did. It also had a grand stadium similar to Rome's Colosseum, called the Hippodrome, in which Romans could unwind and take in a chariot race or two. The one major way that Constantinople differed from the old Roman capital is that unlike Rome, which was filled with pagan temples and shrines, Constantinople was home to plenty of churches and monuments to Christianity. From the very beginning, Constantine demonstrated that his interest was in the newer faith of Christianity.

Constantine saw himself as a protector of the church, and it wasn't long before he was also expected to be an arbiter in church disputes. In the early days of Christianity, there were many disagreements over precisely what official church doctrine should be. There was much confusion, for example, over the nature of the divinity of Christ. Some claimed that Jesus, as the son of God, did not have the same level of authority as God; others claimed that Jesus and God were one and the same, with Jesus merely being a manifestation of God in the flesh.

As these arguments and disagreements grew, Constantine called for a council to be convened in the city of Nicaea in 325. It was here that the so-called Nicene Creed was developed in which it was determined that "Christ and God are of the same substance." This was a major milestone in the streamlining of church belief, turning it into a solid doctrine-based institution over what had been several disagreeing factions. This allowed the concept of the trinity as Christians know it today to be made the prevailing belief.

Yet even while Constantine was playing this vital role for Christianity, some of his own personal actions were decidedly un-Christian. The following year, in 326, he had his wife, Fausta, killed. It remains unclear exactly why Constantine was so ruthless with his wife. According to one account, Fausta had accused Constantine's eldest son Crispus—a son Constantine had fathered with another woman, Minervina—of making sexual advances toward her. Constantine was infuriated, and in his rage, he had his son killed. Shortly thereafter, Constantine apparently learned from his mother that Fausta had made the whole thing up.

Horrified that Fausta had engineered the demise of her own stepson, Constantine then took action against her. Constantine is said to have dropped Fausta in a vat of heated water and had her boiled to death. Other accounts contend that she was strangled in a steam bath. At any rate, whatever may have happened, no one ever talked about Fausta or Crispus ever again, and their names suddenly disappeared from historical mention.

It was immediately after Constantine had two of his family members killed that his mother Helena decided it would be best if she left the capital to visit Israel—or as the Romans called it, the Province of Palestine—in order to retrace the steps of Jesus. Some say that perhaps she was there to do penance for her son's actions.

Helena was said to have been rather generous during her trip, offering alms to the poor and distributing donations in abundance. But Helena wasn't just there for quiet prayer and charity; she was also there to begin some major construction projects. Under her charge, the Church of the Nativity was built in Bethlehem to commemorate the birth of Christ, as well as the Church of Eleona on the Mount of Olives where Christ is said to have ascended to heaven after his resurrection. Both have since become long-lasting bulwarks of the Christian faith.

Not to be outdone, Constantine also commissioned the building of churches, among them the Holy Sepulcher on the outskirts of Jerusalem, which was said to have been the site of Christ's tomb. And, it wasn't just in the Holy Land that grand churches were being built; Constantine was also the driving force behind two of the most famous basilicas in Rome. Although Constantine viewed Constantinople as his capital, he knew from Christian lore that both Saint Peter and Saint Paul—perhaps the two most important figures in Christianity after Jesus—were martyred in Rome. Constantine realized that the sites of their martyrdom were important markers of the faith and tracked down the exact spots where these two Christian martyrs were believed to have died.

This resulted in the building of the Basilica of San Paulo fuori le Mura, or as it would be known in English, Saint Paul Outside the Walls, as well as the now incredibly famous Saint Peter's Basilica. Saint Peter's Basilica, which is now a centerpiece of the Catholic faith, is said to have been built right over the final resting place of Saint Peter in the Vatican City. The fact that the basilica was built on top of Peter's bones has led some Christians to believe that Constantine fulfilled one of Christ's most famous prophecies. In the Bible, Jesus told Peter, "And I say also unto thee, that thou art Peter, and upon this rock I will build my church; and the gates of hell shall not prevail against it."

The name "Peter" was a nickname that Jesus gave to his disciple Simon, thereafter sometimes referred to as "Simon Peter." Jesus spoke Aramaic and most likely would have used the word "*kepa*" which means "rock." The New Testament was originally written in Greek, however, so it used the Greek word for "rock" which is "*petros*." Later translations eventually evolved into the use of "Peter." At any rate, Jesus nicknamed Simon (Saint Peter) "rock," and he told him that "upon this rock," he would build his church.

Since many believe that Constantine did, in fact, build Saint Peter's Basilica on top of Saint Peter's bones—and Saint Peter's Basilica just so happens to be the focal point of the Catholic Church—one could very well argue that Constantine fulfilled the prophecy.

Chapter Five

Reforms and Conquests

*"I profess the most holy religion; and this
worship I declare to be that which teaches me
deeper acquaintance with the most holy God."*

—Constantine the Great

Along with establishing Christianity as the
religion of his realm, Constantine was still very
much concerned with temporal power as well.
Although he had succeeded in rising to the top as
Roman emperor, he knew that all it took for
him—or his designated successor—to be toppled
was the intrigue of a powerful general. It was an
all too common occurrence of the later Roman
Empire to have powerful military generals decide
to take their chances and seize power for
themselves, which led to countless civil wars and
a perpetual state of unrest.

The Tetrarchy was Diocletian's answer to these problems. Diocletian believed that dividing the empire into four main regions controlled by two senior emperors and two junior caesars would reduce the possibility of generals rising up to take over. Constantine had obviously experienced the flaws and limitations of this system firsthand. It was in contemplating how better to safeguard against insurrection that Constantine realized just how important separation of powers in governance was. In the past, the governors of Roman provinces were military generals. This meant that the governor of Britain or Gaul had their own mighty armies at their disposal and could very well decide to send them to Rome in a bid to seize power.

This situation was altogether untenable. Constantine realized that it was the fact that governors had military power that so much unrest was occurring. It was then that he had a stroke of genius in concluding that he should separate political and military power. This meant that the governors of provinces should have a strictly political, civic role and that the generals of the military should not directly control any province. No longer would there be military governors with sizeable armies lurking in every province. With this clever move, the military was essentially centralized under Constantine's sovereign rule.

As neat as it may sound, however, it had the unforeseen side effect of creating massive bureaucratic red tape any time anything needed to be done. If, for example, Germanic tribes to the north were raiding villages in Gaul, the non-military governor had to waste precious time requesting aid. In the past, when military governors reigned supreme, the governor would just send in their own personal, regional legions to stop the incursions. Now there was a lag in communication between the political sphere and the military one. Today, with rapid-fire communication, it's relatively easy for separate branches of government to communicate, but in Constantine's day, when messages rode on horseback, it was much more difficult and time-consuming.

Nevertheless, Constantine remained a big believer in bureaucracy for, under his reign, he presided over the creation of several bureaucratic posts, such as the designation of official counts who oversaw the revenue of the empire, as well as a new master of the offices, which in turn oversaw the counts.

Perhaps the most dramatic institutional reform of Constantine was the fact that he inflated the traditional body of senators in the Roman Senate, from 600 to a whopping 2,000. The Roman Senate had been around since the early days of the Roman Republic, and although Constantine had respect for the senators, he was wary of their machinations. Instead of abolishing the institution, Constantine simply inflated their number. He did this not to give them strength but rather to weaken their influence; 2,000 conflicting Senators could hardly agree on what to eat for lunch, let alone any meaningful policies for the empire.

Just like any other Roman emperor, Constantine desired to expand his power by enlarging his dominion. It was in the year 328, when Constantine was in his fifties, that he went so far as to construct a bridge in Romania, spanning the entire expanse of the Danube River, to invade the previously lost Roman territory in the region of Dacia. In the past, the material wealth of Dacia had provided a great source of revenue for the empire, but Constantine ended up spending so much money in the process of subduing it that his gains were just about worthless.

At any rate, after subduing Dacia, Constantine traveled up to Trier, a Rhineland town which today is part of southwestern Germany. He remained in the region during the fall and winter of 328/329, before moving on to the city of Sirmium, located in modern-day Serbia, in the spring of 329. By May, he had moved on again, this time to Naissus, the town in which he was born, which records state he visited on May 13, 329. Constantine then spent much of the late summer and fall of 329 in Thrace and Heraclea, where he commissioned a mint to create several silver and gold coins. After wintering in Serdica, he then returned to Constantinople in the spring of 330, just in time to officially dedicate the great city as his capital on May 11, 330.

It was at this point that the old Greek settlement previously known as Byzantium was officially given the name Constantinople. Constantine was eager for his new capital to grow but was disappointed that the population at this point was only around 50,000. In contrast, Rome boasted a population of one million people. It would take some time, but Constantine's city would eventually grow to surpass the glories of old Rome altogether.

Chapter Six

Conforming to Constantine's Christianity

"Let us free our life from errors and with the help of the mercy of God, let us direct it along the right path."

—Constantine the Great

By 332, Constantine was on the march once again. He led his armies in battle against both the Sarmatians, as well as the Germanic tribe known as the Goths. The Goths were sorely defeated in these series of skirmishes, dying as much from hunger and disease as they did from Roman swords. In all, it is said that almost 100,000 of their number perished during Constantine's campaign against them.

Constantine was so pleased with the expedition that he took on the title Gothicus

Maximus II and commemorated the event by having gold medallions made, which depicted Constantine vanquishing a Goth and which were emblazoned with the words "*Debellator Gentium Barbarum*," or "Conqueror of the Barbarians." To ensure that the Goths didn't rise up against the empire again, Constantine was also sure to construct several formidable forts all along the Danube River to keep watch on the wildlands of the north.

As successful as Constantine was in the field, however, there was turmoil brewing on the domestic front. Much infighting had emerged in the nascent Roman Catholic Church that Constantine had helped to establish. In particular, a preacher by the name of Arius had begun his own doctrine in North Africa which emphasized that Christ had a beginning since he was known as the son of God, whereas God was an eternal being with no beginning and no end—in other words, the only thing in existence that has existed eternally. Arius' teaching threw a wrench in the doctrine of the trinity, which taught that God, Christ, and the Holy Spirit were all equal members of the trinity. His views managed to get him kicked out of Egypt's Alexandrian Church, and in 332, he was demanding that Constantine have him readmitted.

Constantine, like any Roman emperor before him, was harsh when it came to insubordination. Although he professed to be a Christian, Constantine didn't hesitate to inflict severe punishment upon those he felt were being rebellious against him. Having that said, he was known to be more lenient with members of the clergy. Arius seems to have taken full advantage of this perceived leniency, with his insistent pestering of Constantine.

The emperor eventually lost his patience with the preacher, however, and fired off a missive in which he declared that Arius was nothing short of the "mouthpiece of Satan" for his divergent doctrine. He then sent off another letter, directed toward the public in general, which dictated what he had in store for the troublesome Arius.

Constantine's letter read in part, "Since Arius has imitated wicked and impious people, it is just that he should undergo similar ignominy. Therefore, just as Porphyry, that enemy of piety, for having composed licentious treatises against religion, found suitable compensation when he was branded with infamy, overwhelmed with reproach, and his blasphemous writings were destroyed; so it shall be with Arius, and those who share his sentiments shall be called Porphyrians, that they may hold the appellation of those whose conduct they have imitated. And in addition to this, let any treatise composed by Arius be consumed by flames, so that not only will his depraved doctrine be suppressed, but also so that no memorial of any kind will be left for him."

Constantine's words were harsh, but he felt it was his duty to make sure that Christianity maintained a uniform doctrine, lest the masses become so terribly confused that the Christian Church would splinter into a multitude of unfathomable sects. Even if it meant burning Arius' works, Constantine was more than ready to do it. Furthermore, if anyone were caught with the illegal texts, they could very well pay the price with their lives.

Arius himself was ordered to have an audience with the emperor so that the final outcome of his fate could be determined. On his way to Constantinople, however, Arius collapsed and died. It seems that even though the persecution of Christians in general had ended, there were always those who were willing to come up with different interpretations of mainstream doctrine, and Constantine's government was more than willing to persecute them for daring to do so. Although it was now okay to be a Christian in the Roman Empire, you had to be the right kind of Christian.

Chapter Seven

Taking on the Persians

"How pleasing to the wise and intelligent portion of mankind is the concord which exists among you!"

—Constantine the Great

As his reign neared its end, Constantine felt he had one last major military campaign left to complete. He, like so many other leaders of the Greco-Roman world before him, looked toward the east for conquest. The Persian Empire had long been battling the Greeks, and once Greek lands were swallowed up by the Roman Empire, that task then fell upon the Romans.

Constantine was indeed interested in trying his luck at the Persians as well. Before he could even begin to wage war on them though, he decided to send the Persian king, Shapur II, a letter. In his letter to the Persian monarch, Constantine reaffirmed his belief that his Christian faith would lead him to victory. He also extolled the king to treat Christians under Persian dominion well. This was of particular importance to Constantine in light of the Armenians' conversion to Christianity.

Armenia had adopted Christianity as its official religion all the way back in 301 CE. The progress of Armenian Christians had been disrupted, however, when Shapur II ordered his troops to remove the Christian king of Armenia and put a Zoroastrian in his place. Zoroastrianism was the ancestral faith of Persia, and before the lands of modern-day Iran were converted to Islam, the Persian people were by and large Zoroastrians. During the days of Shapur II, it was the Zoroastrians of his kingdom that were the most favored religious group. So it was that Shapur II sought to put a Zoroastrian on the Armenian throne. In addition, Shapur II was known to launch persecutions against regular Christians living within his domain.

Shapur was not easily deterred, and after subsequent border raids launched by the Persians against the eastern frontiers of the Roman Empire, Constantine decided to have his son Constantius lead a legion of troops to safeguard the east in 335. Unfortunately, this didn't help the Armenians much since Persian forces stormed into Armenia the following year, in 336. It was that year that Persian Prince Narseh waylaid the Armenians and forced them to put a Persian-friendly despot on the Armenian throne. This was the last straw as far as Constantine was concerned, and he prepared to go to war against Persia, which in many ways had all the hallmarks of a religious-tinged crusade.

There were Christians within the Persian Empire who very much did look toward Constantine as their great Christian crusader who would come and rescue them from the tyranny of the Persians. According to writer and biographer Paul Stephenson, a Christian resident of the Persian Empire, whose name comes down to us as Aphrahat, even began proclaiming that the biblical Book of Daniel had predicted that "the Persians would be cast down by the Romans, whose empire would persist until the end times, when its powers would be surrendered to Christ."

Constantine, for one, was ready to agree with this assertion. He did indeed see himself as the vanguard of Christianity and perhaps even a man destined to fulfill the will the God. Along with all of the prophetic Christian imagery, Constantine was also rather fond of likening himself to the ancient Macedonian pagan Alexander the Great.

Alexander the Great had successfully conquered the Persian Empire several centuries prior. Constantine saw himself as following in Alexander's footsteps, and perhaps he would have, if only he had been able to live long enough to do so.

Chapter Eight

The Death of the Emperor

"I myself, brethren, am disposed to love you with an enduring affection, inspired both by religion, and by your own manner of life and zeal on my behalf."

—Constantine the Great

Constantine left Constantinople in early 337 to visit the city he had named after his mother, Helenopolis. His health was now beginning to fail him, yet after this brief stop, he made his way to the city of Nicomedia with his army right behind. His main body of troops made an encampment outside of the city while Constantine hobnobbed with regional officials and other persons of interest—one of which was the local bishop, Eusebius.

It was in front of Eusebius that Constantine surprised everyone by announcing his intention to be baptized. Constantine had been an openly practicing Christian for some time, but he had yet to be baptized. Since baptism was believed to absolve one of their sins, it seems that Constantine was purposefully waiting until the end of his life so that he could be as sin-free as possible when he finally passed on.

Constantine gave an impassioned speech about these developments, stating, "This is the moment I have long hoped for, as I thirsted and yearned to win salvation in God. It is our time to enjoy the seal that brings immortality, time to enjoy the sealing that gives salvation, which I once intended to receive at the streams of the River Jordan, where our Saviour is reported also to have received the bath as an example to us. But God who knows what is good for us judges us worthy of these things here and now."

After his baptism, it became clear to all that Constantine was living on borrowed time. It is said that once this realization was made, his subordinates were quite discouraged as to the future of the realm. According to Eusebius' later recollection, "When the tribunes and senior officers of the armies filed in and lamented, bewailing their own imminent bereavement and wishing him longer life, he answered them too by saying he enjoyed true life now, and only he knew the good things he had received."

While his troops were awaiting their commander to send them headlong into Persia, Constantine succumbed to the increasing frailty of his health, passing away on May 22, 337. Word that Constantine had died was sent to the city of Antioch, in Asia Minor, where Constantine's son Constantius was located at the time. In those days, messages were carried by way of horse stations. A station was situated every few miles, and a messenger would switch horses at every station so that a fresh, well-rested, and fast horse could be used to expedite the delivery of a message. This was the means by which news of Constantine's passing traveled hundreds of miles from Nicomedia to Antioch.

As soon as he learned of his father's death, Constantius made his way to his father's side to see to his last rites. Many were concerned that the Persians would strike while Constantius was distracted by his deceased father's affairs, but this was not the case. For whatever reason, Shapur II decided to stay his hand. The Roman army, parked at Nicomedia, was essentially running itself until Constantius came along to restore order in the ranks.

Constantine's body was then taken back to Constantinople. It's said that he was shed of his baptismal robes and instead placed back into his royal raiment of gold and purple. The emperor's body lay in state for several days while well-wishers came to see their liege one last time. Constantine's final resting place was an officially commissioned mausoleum in Constantinople. This fact apparently angered citizens in Rome, who rioted when they learned that the Roman emperor would not have his final resting place in Rome. This was especially aggravating since Constantine had pledged to have his remains interred in a mausoleum just outside of Rome. His mother Helena had been interred there when she passed in 329, so it was naturally assumed that her son would be placed there as well.

Today it might seem odd for people to be so concerned over where the bones of one of their great leaders were interred, but in those days, the symbolism of the final depository of royal remains meant everything. The city that housed the emperor's mortal remains was considered the true capital of the empire, and the fact that Rome began to decline from this point forward while Constantinople began its rapid ascent would only seem to lend credence to this view.

At any rate, the succession of Constantine went forward, and it was the job of the military generals to make sure that the claimants to the throne were secure. In order to avoid chaos among the masses, they kept a tight lid on many of the developments that were underway in the immediate aftermath of Constantine's demise. Prefects and other officials even continued to rubber stamp various bits of legislation in Constantine's name in the first three months after his death.

In the end though, the leadership of the Roman Empire would have to be hammered out between Constantine's three surviving sons—Constantine II, Constantius, and Constans. These three brothers all met with each other in September of 337 and divided the empire up amongst each other, with all three becoming declared emperors by the Roman Senate on September 9. In this arrangement, Constantius would have the lion's share of territory, holding most of the eastern half of the empire. Constans would control Italy and North Africa, while Constantine II would control Gaul, Britain, and the Iberian Peninsula. It wouldn't be long, however, before fractures in this arrangement would emerge.

In 340, Constantine II sent his troops into Constans' territory, and fighting erupted. Constantine II perished in this skirmish. This left Constans in full control of the west while his remaining brother Constantius had control of the east. Constantius, for his part, was not willing to challenge his brother since he had his hands full with Persia. Constantius would be focused on this task for the next several years.

This status quo did not change until 350 when Constans was overthrown in a coup and ultimately murdered. Constantius was able to rise against the usurpers, defeat them, and become the sole emperor of the Roman Empire in 353—a reign that would last until his death in 361.

Conclusion

Constantine the Great is known for many things. He was a great and powerful Roman emperor, one of the last to successfully rule the great expanse of the empire of his own accord. He was also arguably the most pivotal instrument—aside from the apostles themselves—in the spread of Christianity. Through official edicts, Constantine helped spread toleration of Christianity throughout the empire and then became a full-blown promoter of the faith when he made it the official religion of the realm.

Constantine's reason for doing all of this, if you believe the testimony of Constantine himself, was because of a mystical vision that had been imparted to him, in which he was told that it was through the cross that he would conquer. Others have a more cynical view of Constantine's motives and have suggested that he simply tapped into what he already knew was a powerful movement for his own political benefit.

At any rate, Constantine was indeed a successful military commander and went on to become a successful imperial ruler. If he hadn't been triumphant in these ventures, his claims would not have been the least bit believable, but it was precisely because he was so successful that his claims of divine inspiration took hold among the masses. Thanks to that, Constantine was able to tap into the popular sentiment of the time and rally his people to causes greater than himself.

In fact, he spent his last year of life rallying them to what would have been the greatest campaign of his career—taking on the Persian Empire. Constantine had received word that Christians were being mistreated by the Persians, and he was ready to go on what was tantamount to a crusade when he suddenly fell irreparably ill. Realizing the end was near, he decided to get baptized and prepare himself to meet his maker. Constantine the Great, never one to shy away from his destiny, marched full steam ahead into the unknown.

Bibliography

Barnes, Timothy (2011). *Constantine: Dynasty, Religion and Power in the Later Roman Empire.*

Corcoran, Simon (1996). *The Empire of the Tetrarchs: Imperial Pronouncements and Government, AD 284-324.*

Dillon, John (2012). *The Justice of Constantine: Law, Communication, and Control.*

Matthews, John (2021). *Empire of the Romans: From Julius Caesar to Justinian: Six Hundred Years of Peace and War.*

Morgan, Julian (2003). *Constantine: Ruler of Christian Rome.*

Stephenson, Paul (2009). *Constantine: Roman Emperor, Christian Victor.*